Contents

3		Letter from the Co-Authors
4		A Stigmatized Story
5		Prisonworld – Where Are The Jobs For Felons
6		Jobs For Felons Books/Workshops
7		The Felon Job Market
8-9		FYI
10-11		Help Wanted
12		Start Your Own Business
13		How To Start A Food Truck Business
14		How To Start A Recycling Business
15		How To start a Junk Hauling Business
16 17		
18 - 19		Felons & The Military
20		Illegal Interview Questions
21		Federal Bonding Program
22-23		Sample Resume
		Notes

Future Entrepreneur Network
Jobs for Felons:
From Inmates to Entrepreneurs

Letter from the Co-Authors

To anyone that has made the decision to read this book, not just the formerly incarcerated or those that are employment challenged, anyone that had just an ounce of curiosity to see what this is all about…we thank you.

Change does not always come how we want it or when we want it. It doesn't always come sweet with a cherry on top nor does it come quietly. The movement to stop mass incarceration has become quite a loud movement, so we decided to move in the direction that is not being heard so much. We want to help people re-enter society, get their lives back on track, pay their bills so they can support their children and not use the system as a revolving door.

Our company, Dawah International, LLC has been helping inmates from the inside and outside for almost 10 years. Information is key. Knowledge on how to do many things is imperative for returning citizens. Actually re-entering society from prison is met with so many challenges that this book, Jobs For Felons: From Inmates to Entrepreneurs, is just the tip of the iceberg on what the Future Entrepreneur Network is doing or capable of doing. But just like with anything, baby steps. Volume I is the tester, the flagship. It will tell us where we stand with the general public as to where more information and resources are needed. Aren't you happy you took the steps to be a part of a phenomenal movement!

Jenny & Rufus Triplett
Co-Owners of Dawah International, LLC
www.dawahinc.com

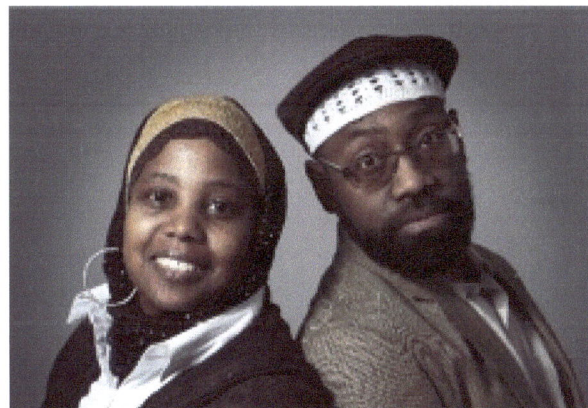

Future Entrepreneur Network
Jobs for Felons:
From Inmates to Entrepreneurs

The Stigmatized Story

P An excerpt form a story in the American Prospect Magazine regarding how ex-offenders are stigmatized and let out of the job pool upon release.

risonworld Magazine is a known source for information on prisoners and the prison system. The co-editors and co-publishers have provided valuable information for media sources across the country and around the world. One of the latest was for The American Prospect Magazine.

Excerpt is as follows:

Motivating those efforts are cases like that of 40-year-old Glenn Martin. In 1995, he was convicted for an armed robbery of a New York City jewelry store and was sentenced to six years in prison. When he went to jail, he had $300 in outstanding child-support debt and owed $100 a week as part of his regular court-ordered payment. He was worried because he'd have no income in prison and knew he'd emerge owing more money. He guessed at the time it would total $3,000 or $4,000.

When he got out in June 2001, he decided to turn his life around, get a job, and stay out of trouble. But then he found out about his child-support bill. Not only had his payments accrued during the six years but the state had tacked on 9 percent compounding interest. The bill was $50,000.

Two months after being out, he landed a $17,000-a-year job answering phones for a nonprofit law firm. At that salary, he knew he'd never get out from under his debt. So he got the money the only way he knew how. He won't say what he did but calls it "unmentionable" and says if he'd gotten caught, he would have ended up back in prison and still be there today.

Martin is not a rare case. Jenny Triplett, publisher of the Georgia-based magazine Prisonworld, which is distributed inside jails, often talks to ex-prisoners who seek job advice and contacts. Like Ohio, Georgia considers prisoners to be voluntarily unemployed and makes paying child-support debt a condition of their probation. Triplett says trying to meet that probation requirement is, perversely, often what leads them back to crimes like dealing drugs. "They'll say to me, which I don't like to hear, 'I just have to go do what I know,' and they revert back to what they know with a quick sell."

While there are no current national figures on child-support debt among prisoners, a 2002 estimate showed that a sample of Massachusetts inmates would leave prison in arrears by an average of $31,000; in Colorado the figure among a group of parolees in 2001 was $16,700. Until Michigan launched a project to adjust prisoners' debts in 2004, inmates owed an average of $28,000, according to figures from the state's Supreme Court.

Prisonworld

Magazine ©
November/December 2011

Where Are The Jobs For Felons?

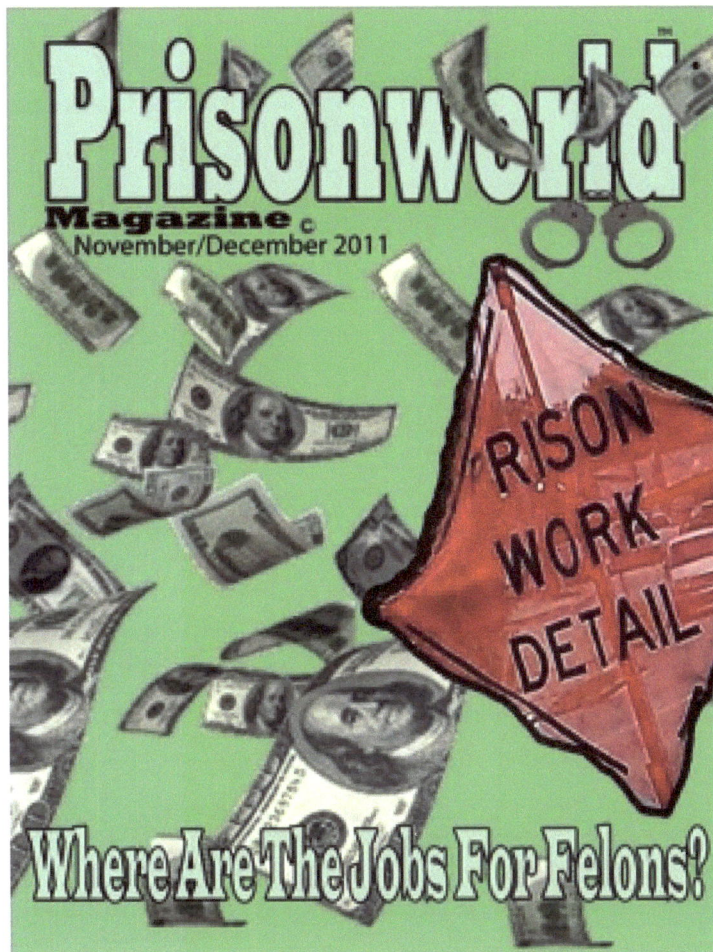

Felon, felony, criminal record, ex-offender, ex-con, etc., etc., etc. These labels in the job market are a hindrance. They are a separating factor of who gets in and who goes in File 13 even before an interview. Once an individual had completed their time of incarceration, they are further subjected to pre-employment biases and hiring manager judgments many years after the court imposed sentence is said and done.

Prisoner re-entry is not new to the Triplett's who are certified Georgia prison volunteers. Their work and reach extends inside and outside the prison system so they remain truly in tune with the needs of those coming out of the system. Not only are Jenny and Rufus a husband and wife team in 25 plus years of marriage as showcased in their best-selling book *Surviving Marriage in the 21st Century*, but also as business partners. "There appears to be a lot of people fighting to stop mass incarceration. That's great. But the fight is twofold. The fact still remains that several people are incarcerated and return to incarceration because they don't get the help they need on the outside. That's where we come in with providing valuable resources and reliable information. The majority of the information provided to inmates inside the system as to what is available outside the system for them, is wrong. We clear that up and help them move forward. We get companies and organizations to see how they can help. The more we encourage people to stop judging those that have been formerly incarcerated and think outside the box, they actually understand what we are trying to do," says Jenny Triplett, co-Editor-in Chief of the magazine.

Future Entrepreneur Network
Jobs for Felons:
From Inmates to Entrepreneurs

5

Prisonworld Magazine has been in print since 2007, ships domestically and internationally, was recognized by the White House as a "creative form of media" and a letter of acknowledgement from President Obama as well as numerous other recognitions for community work and activism. **Jobs for Felons** workshops stemmed from the idea of the Triplett's book, *Future Entrepreneur Network – Jobs for Felons: From Inmates to Entrepreneurs,* to be released July 2016. While teaching inmates to tune into and develop their entrepreneurship skills while incarcerated, upon release they may not be able to immediately start their ventures. Parole and probation require steady employment and that is where the cycle of continuous struggle to secure employment begins.

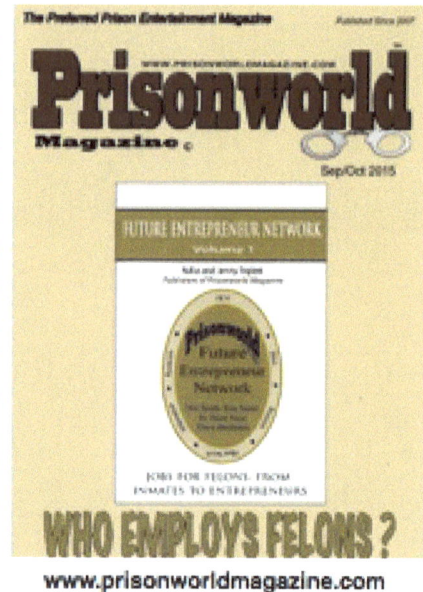

www.prisonworldmagazine.com

"That little box on employment applications "have you ever been convicted of a crime" stops so many people from getting a fair chance. Employers see that and move on to the next applicant. The Ban the Box movement has helped but employers may and can discriminate in other ways. We teach the skills needed to be better prepared, push past the application to obtain an interview, how to dress, how to interview and how to talk about your previous incarceration in order to present yourself for job opportunities. You can always work on your own ideas while working a job to make sure you stay in compliance with the terms of your release," says Rufus Triplett, co-Editor-in-Chief.

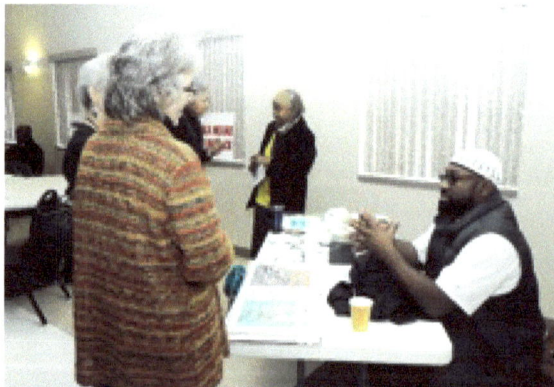

Jobs for Felons Workshops

Jenny and Rufus Triplett appear at many functions to spread the word about how every day people can help with those that are formerly incarcerated succeed in life.

Seen here at a conference in Buffalo, NY, the Tripletts take time to speak with every individual, hear their stories and situations and provide answers as best as possible.

Although information may vary from state to state, plenty resources are the same just with a different name.

Spreading the Word

As more people are released from the system, the need is great to get the word to the masses about how to properly re-enter society. Laws are changing, slowly, to give a second/fair chance, but not fast enough to slow the cycle of recidivism,.

Future Entrepreneur Network
Jobs for Felons:
From Inmates to Entrepreneurs

The Felon Job Market

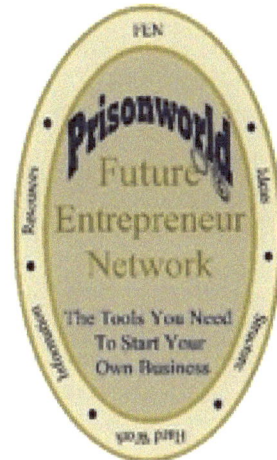

- Currently the job market is tough for those without a criminal record. Coming out of prison with a criminal record and being required to find a job is a crime within itself. The average ex-offender has multiple obstacles in finding a job. Knowing how, knowing where, and knowing what is legally available to you is a step in the right direction. You are already stigmatized by many for being a convicted felon. But the point is not to remain stuck in your situation. Move on and move forward.

- After working countless hours in prison jobs (i.e. the kitchen, the dog program, P.I., mechanics, landscaping, orderlies, etc.) you acquire various skills. Finding someone to respect your skills and how you acquired them is a completely different story. Hopefully the following is a help to you and brings you hope.

- **Why I Hire Former Convicts and Gang Members**

- When I took over Electronic Recyclers International in late 2004, it was a failing company. I decided to restructure and rebrand it. And when it came time to hire new employees, I saw an opportunity to hire individuals from what have typically been marginalized segments of society: former convicts, former gang members, the homeless, people recovering from drug addiction, and people coming off of welfare.

Finding the right job is hard. It can be even harder for people with a criminal record. Ex-offenders must pay special consideration to how they write their resume, answer interview questions, and network. There is employment and job training help out there for job seekers with criminal records, but you need to know where to look.

It wasn't the first time I'd hired employees looking for a second chance. Back in 1993, I co-founded Homeboy Tortillas and Homeboy Industries -- two small businesses that train and employ former gang members, helping them transition into the workforce. It was a landmark moment in my life, and from then on, I wanted to make sure any business I took part in had a bottom line for profit *and* for social responsibility. I felt strongly about continuing that mission at the recycling company, which safely dismantles and recycles electronic waste.

Everyone at our company buys into that mission. We posted a quote from Dr. Martin Luther King, Jr. -- "Everyone can be great, because everyone can serve" -- over the front door in all of our regional offices. We all agreed that we need to make money, but also that we can seek to turn people's lives around by opening our doors and our hearts to those in need.

Having a criminal record expunged, pardoned, or sealed is not an option for everyone. Knowing more about these proceeding can help you find out what your options might be. Some ex-offenders are able to get all or part of their criminal records cleared so it is no longer a barrier to their job search. The information below is for informational purposes only. Talk to a legal professional to find out if you are eligible to have items removed from your record.

Laws for every state differ. There are general laws and federal laws that may apply to all, but to be absolutely sure you should research each individual company to see what their policy is on hiring felons.

Policies and legal standards governing the employment of people with criminal records are created mainly by state laws. However, the Equal Employment Opportunity Commission (EEOC) has ruled that employers governed by Title VII of the Civil Rights Act cannot deny people employment based on arrests that did not lead to conviction unless there is a "business justification"; nor can they deny people employment because of a criminal conviction unless there is a "business necessity." An example of legitimate business necessity might be denying an applicant employment as a bus driver if he or she has a recent conviction for a driving-related offense. But an old drug conviction might not justify denial of employment for a food services job on grounds of "business necessity." Minorities with arrest and conviction records whose civil rights are violated can sue under Title VII.

Employers in most states can deny jobs to people who were arrested but never convicted of any crime.

•Millions of Americans are arrested but not convicted every year. Most people assume that if criminal charges are dropped or if they are found not guilty, records of those arrests will disappear or, at the very least, cannot be used against them when they apply for a job or housing. The facts suggest otherwise:
•• 38 states have laws permitting all employers and occupational licensing agencies to ask about and consider arrests that never led to conviction in making employment decisions.
•• Only 10 states prohibit all employers and occupational licensing agencies from considering arrests if the arrest did not lead to conviction, and 3 states prohibit some employers and occupational licensing agencies from doing so.

Future Entrepreneur Network
Jobs for Felons:
From Inmates to Entrepreneurs

Although Georgia has Banned the Box there are several other discriminations that take place during the hiring process.

Governor Deal Signs 'Ban the Box' Hiring Policy

via AJC.com

By Greg Bluestein

Job seekers applying for work with the state of Georgia will no longer need to disclose prior criminal convictions on their initial applications.

Gov. Nathan Deal signed an executive order implementing a "ban the box" policy that outlaws a requirement for people with criminal histories to disclose that information on a job form.

"Such policies will allow returning citizens an opportunity to explain their unique circumstances in person to a potential employer," read the order.

The initiative was recommended by Deal's criminal justice reform council in January 2014. The council's report said it was a barrier to employment that could exclude released inmates from consideration even if they are qualified for the job and the conviction has no bearing on the work.

It urged instead a requirement that the applicant disclose any criminal history during a face-to-face interview with the hiring agent.

Deal has long suggested he would sign an order banning state agencies from including the question as part of broader criminal justice changes aimed at helping released inmates transition more smoothly back into society.

"If they can find employment, if they can find a place to live, I believe many of them will work hard to earn their place in society," Deal said in an April 2013 speech outlining the next phase of his criminal justice reform plan.

About 97 percent of those sentenced to prison in Georgia will eventually be released, and more than 1,300 re-enter society each month without employment, according to Deal's office.

The city of Atlanta in October endorsed similar procedures. And 13 states have adopted the policy, including New Mexico, New Jersey and Minnesota. Georgia would be the first state in the South to implement the initiative, Deal's office said.

The order requires state agencies to offer qualified applicants the chance in a follow-up interview to "contest the content and relevance of a criminal record" and provide information that demonstrates rehabilitation.

It carves out exceptions for those seeking "sensitive governmental positions" in which a criminal history would be an immediate disqualification. That includes jobs such as prison guards or security officers.

Employers in most states can deny jobs to – or fire- anyone with a criminal record, regardless of individual history, circumstance, or "business necessity."

•Most states permit employers to deny jobs across the board to anyone who has been convicted of a crime or a certain category of crime, without considering the circumstances of the offense, its relevance to the job, the amount of time that has elapsed, the job being sought, evidence of rehabilitation, or the "business necessity" for barring the applicant, in potential violation of EEOC guidelines.

•• 26 states have no standards governing the relevance of conviction records of applicants for occupational licenses. That means they can deny licenses based on any criminal conviction, regardless of history, circumstance or business necessity; 25 states do have standards that require a "direct," "rational," or "reasonable" relationship between the license sought and the applicant's criminal history.

•• 34 states have no standards governing public employers

•• 43 states have no standards governing private employers; 8 do

The Central Park Five. (from L to R) Yusuf Salaam, Korey Wise, Antron McCray, Kevin Richardson, Raymond Santana, wrongly convicted of rape.

States have the power to offer certificates of rehabilitation but few issue them.
Employers in a growing number of professions, including home health care, nursing, education, eyeglass dispensing, plumbing, and even barbering, are barred by state licensing agencies from hiring people with a wide range of criminal convictions, even convictions which are unrelated to the job or license sought. All states have the power to lift those bars to employment by offering certificates of rehabilitation or some other form of restoration of rights in addition to pardons. Yet only 9 states -- Alabama, Arizona, California, Connecticut Hawaii, Iowa, Illinois, New Jersey and New York -- offer restoration of civil rights/certificates of rehabilitation for employment or occupational licensing purposes.

When companies are hiring, felons are not first to get the jobs

These jobs will be hard to fill in 2012 and definitely not by those being released from prison.

Although the economy continues to face many challenges, the startup and tech industries are very much alive. The IPO window slightly opened up for companies like LinkedIn, Pandora, Groupon, Zynga, and Carbonite. We saw monster rounds of funding for companies like Facebook, Twitter, Dropbox. The appetite for seed and angel investing was extremely active. Tech incubators and accelerator programs kept popping up.

A look back at the job market in 2012:

It was also a very busy year for hiring at startup companies, as you know, and it doesn't look like that will slow down in 2012. We've certainly seen opinions on both sides of the fence as to whether or not there is a tech bubble or 2012 will be another active year of investing. I'm an optimist and I believe the pace of investing will remain consistent. Yes, some companies will fail, of course, but others will scale and grow their teams at a steady clip.

Hiring the best of the best is an absolute must if you are going to build a successful company. You will need to be prepared to compete against big companies with deep pockets and other up-and-coming startups that also have blue chip investors and a game-changing idea.

So, what are the most competitive areas for talent these days? Take a look on the next page.

Software Engineers and Web Developers

The demand for top-tier engineering talent sharply outweighs the supply in almost every market especially in San Francisco, New York, and Boston. This is a major, major pain point and problem that almost every company is facing, regardless of the technology "stack" their engineers are working on.

Creative Design and User Experience

After engineers, the biggest challenge for companies is finding high-quality creative design and user-experience talent. Since almost every company is trying to create a highly compelling user experience that keeps people engaged with their product, it is tough to find people who have this type of experience (especially with mobile devices including tablets) and a demonstrated track record of success.

Product Management

It is always helpful for an early-stage company to hire someone who has very relevant and specific experience in your industry. This is especially true for product management, since the person in this role will interface with customers and define the product strategy and use cases. However, be prepared, as it will be a challenge to find people with experience in these high-growth industries: consumer web, e-commerce, mobile, software as a service, and cloud computing.

Jenny and Rufus Triplett speaking to a room full of formerly incarcerated people

Future Entrepreneur Network
Jobs for Felons:
From Inmates to Entrepreneurs

Marketing

I'm not talking about old-school marketing communications. Companies are looking for expert online marketers who know how to create a buzz of inbound marketing or viral traffic through the web, social media, and content discovery. Writing a good press release just doesn't cut it anymore, as everyone is looking for the savvy online marketing professional who understands how the current state of the web operates and knows how to make it work to their benefit.

Analytics

Since data is becoming more and more accessible, smart companies are increasingly making decisions driven by metrics. Analytics is becoming a central hub across companies where everything (web, marketing, sales, operations) is being measured and each decision is supported by data. Thus, we are seeing a high level of demand for analytics and business intelligence professionals who almost act like internal consultants; they help determine what should be measured and then build out the capability for a company.

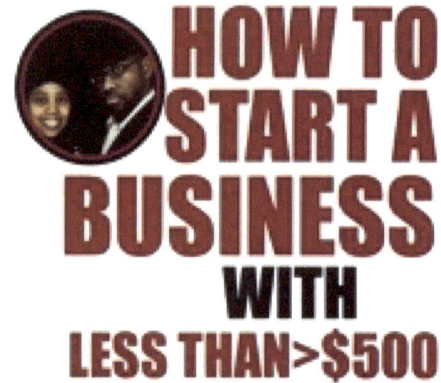

HOW TO START A BUSINESS WITH LESS THAN >$500

Webinar Hosted by Entrepreneurial Couple
RUFUS & JENNY

www.rufusandjennytriplett.com

Webinars are a great way of creating passive income.

What's passive income? As per Google –

Passive income is an income received on a regular basis, with little effort required to maintain it. The American Internal Revenue Service categorizes income into three broad types, active income, passive income, and portfolio income.

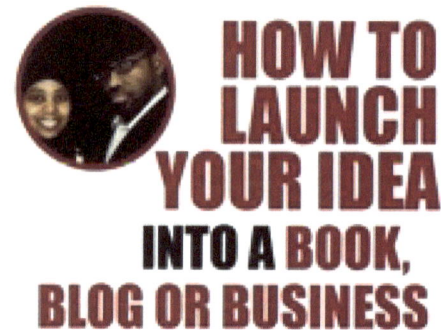

HOW TO LAUNCH YOUR IDEA INTO A BOOK, BLOG OR BUSINESS

Webinar Hosted by Entrepreneurial Couple
RUFUS & JENNY

www.rufusandjennytriplett.com

From Behind the Screen to In Front of the Scene

A webinar can also be turned into a live presentation or speaking engagement. Content is king. Once you master the art of creating content, you will always find an audience that is seeking your knowledge.

Future Entrepreneur Network
Jobs for Felons:
From Inmates to Entrepreneurs

Food Trucks 101: How to Start a Mobile Food Business

A new generation of street food lovers are lining up at food trucks and food carts. Though the idea is a long-standing part of American and world culture, the street food industry has never enjoyed so much popularity or publicity.

Chefs can open up shop for much less than a restaurant, and develop simple menus that focus on particular cuisines or ingredients. Fans can follow their favorite trucks on Twitter and sample an assortment of dishes at large gatherings of trucks. Even the Food Network has leapt on the trend with The Great Food Truck Race, which features gourmand trucks like Roxy's Grilled Cheese; Seabirds (vegan cuisine); Spencer on the Go (authentic French foods like escargot); and the season one winner, Grill 'Em All, a heavy-metal themed truck from Los Angeles that serves gourmet hamburgers.

The industry is booming with approximately 3 million food trucks in the U.S., more than 5 million food carts, and an unknown number of kiosks, which have appeared in malls, train and bus stations, airports, stadiums, conference centers and other locations in recent years.

Food industry observers claim that the increase in food truck business is largely in response to the slow-growing economy. People are seeking inexpensive breakfasts and lunches. Also, more employees are often pressed for time, with more work and shorter lunch hours. With new gourmet trucks, foodies can also sample unique dishes for less than a restaurant meal.

From an entrepreneurial standpoint, mobile food businesses have a lower overhead and require fewer employees than restaurants and can be easily moved if one location does not generate enough business.

Here's a quick rundown of nuts and bolts of the food-truck business, including the basics for getting started.

Going Mobile: Your Options
Even before you decide what foods to sell, you'll want to consider how you want to sell them. There are several options, including the ubiquitous food truck; food kiosks (small, temporary food stands in malls, stadiums, airports and other locations); food carts that sell pre-prepared or easy-to-prepare food like hot dogs and ice cream; and catering trucks. A new option is "bustaurants," refurbished double-decker buses where patrons dine on the second level.

A decision on how to sell your foods will depend on:

Your startup budget and potential for returns
Your commitment to the business: part or full time
Your creative ideas and what it will take to fulfill them
The type of food you wish to prepare
Your experience at running a business
The size of the business you want to start
Your ideal demographic

HOW TO START A BUSINESS for UNDER $500

Do you like organizing cluttered garages? Do you make mouth-watering cakes? Do you love to make jewelry? Are you good at planning special events? If you've been thinking about starting a business as your next career, now could be a great time to turn one of these hobbies into a thriving small business -- even on a bare-bones budget.

Starting a business on the side is a smart way to get your feet wet as an entrepreneur. Look first at the services and goods you already provide for free to friends and family. "The best way to start a business for less than $500 is to figure out how to get paid for what you love to do," says Clyde Anderson, a financial lifestyle coach and CNN contributor in Atlanta. "It's crucial for anyone who's looking to start a business to determine what gifts and talents they already have and to convert them into an actual business."

Here is one cool business to start on a shoestring.

1. Baker
Cakes and cupcakes are the highlight of any party, and reality foodie shows such as Cupcake Wars have made baking a popular new business idea. Brooklyn blogger and cupcake expert Nichelle Stephens says you can start a cupcake business for $500 or less, as long as you aren't trying to open a storefront. "You spend more time than money when starting a baking business," says Stephens, who shares baking and business tips on her blog. "You need to find a neighborhood where there is a limited number of baked goods available and identify your niche." Once you get your mixer, the next expense is quality baking pans and cooling racks. Use your co-workers as your test market and promote your business in the groups you belong to, especially if you have children. Other parents are a great potential customer base. Keep in mind it's illegal in most jurisdictions to bake and sell food from your home. Here's a website where you can research commercial kitchens in your area.

The President's Job Act is making headlines all across America. Republican and Democrats alike are hiding their heads in the sand and neglecting the issues while the American people continue to suffer. One class of people are suffering more than others and more than usual...felons. There tends to be a lack of outlets for people with criminal records to get a job. Now that the competition is super stiff, felons have to compete with those that have masters degrees and PhD's. Inmates need to become entrepreneurs and not depend on American society for work. We help stigmatized felons with ways become entrepreneurs and not use the system as a revolving door. Here is one great idea:

HOW TO START YOUR OWN PAPER RECYCLING BUSINESS

One of the easiest – and in fact one of the oldest ways of making extra money – is by collecting old newspapers and selling them to a recycling plant in your locale. Some paper recyclers are making more than $100,000 a year in this business. If other people are doing it, then there's no reason you can't do it. About the only equipment you'll need is a pickup truck or trailer that you can pull along behind your personal car. The prices you would be paid would astound you.

Make no mistake about it; we live in a paper world. American uses 200 million tons of paper each year. After quick use, we throw away at least 100 million tons of this paper, almost all of which could be recycled. This means that there's about 8 million dollars worth of paper out there that can be collected and recycled each year. So if you are looking to start a business with real profit potential, what are you waiting for?

In the beginning, you may have to make up a sign and tape it to the side of your pick-up or car, and pound the pavement, but you would expect to do this in starting any business. You should organize your time and schedule to call upon all business owners, store managers and ask them if you can haul away their old cardboard boxes. Another paper products source: the offices in your area, particularly those with computers. The age of computers has ushered in more reports for offices than ever before, adding reams and reams of paper to the average office trash basket. When you visit these offices, take along a couple of save-a-tree boxes and ask the office people to discard al their waste paper into these boxes for you – letters, envelopes, outdated reports and files. You can usually get the "save-a-tree" boxes at your recycling depot, and when full, we're talking about 35 to 45 pounds of paper. Most offices will fill one of these boxes in a week or two, depending, of course upon their volume of paperwork. And while you're on this kind of foraging trip, don't forget to check in at all the print shops. They waste and throw away almost as much paper as they sell.

This is the kind of business that "snowballs" with visibility and word-of-mouth advertising. It will definitely benefit you, then, to join the various civic and service clubs in your area, attend their luncheons, mingle with the business leaders in your area. Volunteer to assist in some fund-raising events, and whenever possible, become a guest speaker and tell about your business.

This business takes organization, some energy on your part, and at least in the beginning, your time. But if you put forth the effort as I have outlines, there's no reason you shouldn't easily realize a very comfortable income with your own RECYCLING BUSINESS. It takes effort on your part, but if you're looking for a lucrative business, you have here a plan to act on.

JOBS for FELONS - Junk Hauling like Sanford & Son

JUNK HAULING AS A BUSINESS

Junk hauling doesn't sound like a very glamorous job but it can be a very profitable one in the long run. Most people would picture a junk hauler being someone throwing a bunch of trash in the back of an old beat up truck and driving everything to the city dump. In truth there is a much larger business to the junk hauler's life.

Junk hauling is the primary business, but then you have the additional services of offering to clean out attics and basements. This service is a profitable opportunity in more ways than one. First you get paid to clear out all the "junk" from the attic or basement, but what many people throw away can be very profitable – several items could be sold on E-bay. Other items could be of value to antique collectors, and the last is those items having value in recycling. Paper and cardboard, aluminum cans, assorted metals, all can be turned into cash. So, you charge a fee to clean the space out, get paid to haul the "junk" away, and then get paid again by selling what you can.

There is one or two large junk hauling businesses out there today valued in the millions of dollars region. Your small hauling company might, some day, be a large franchise worth millions of dollars if you run It professionally.

Future Entrepreneur Network - From Inmate to Entrepreneur

Everyone was not born to be an entrepreneur, but if you were, you will possess all three of these skills. They are a must for success in just about anything that you do but especially in running your own business.

• **Planner**: Take time to plan your day and your thought process. One of the worst mistakes that you could do is not have a plan. Everything requires a plan, a business plan, a marketing plan, an event plan, etc. A good entrepreneur knows how to plan and foresees the obstacles that may occur.

• **Listener**: Be a good listener. Learn how to listen for the right key words on the phone. Read your emails as if you were having that conversation over the phone or in person. Communication is a two way street. It takes a giver of information and a receiver of information. Whatever end you are on, make sure your ears are open.

• **Presenter**: Know how to present information with the just the right amount of pizazz and enthusiasm. Your audience will feed off of your energy and the energy you create in the room. When you are preparing for a presentation, prepare as if you are performing a show and want to dazzle your audience. Make sure they remember more than just the first and last things you say.

Remember that success is all relative to your passion and your purpose. Focus on what makes you want to get up in the morning and continue the everyday struggle of the entrepreneur. Plan your work and work your plan.

Felony waivers up

The number of Army recruits with felony convictions more than doubled from 2006 to 2007.

Felony conviction waivers

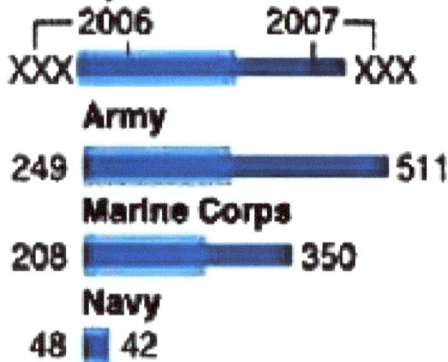

	2006	2007	
Army	XXX		XXX
Marine Corps	249		511
Navy	208		350
	48	42	

SOURCE: The House Oversight and Government Reform Committee   AP

Employment Links:

http://www.hirenetwork.org/
http://www.workforcelink.com/
http://www.bls.gov/oco/
http://www.careeronestop.org/

For Writers:

· www.ezinearticles.com
· www.articledashboard.com
· www.isnare.com
· www.articlebiz.com

Work From Home:

www.alpineaccess.com
www.dorminc.biz

Future Entrepreneur Network
Jobs for Felons:
From Inmates to Entrepreneurs

Q Can a convicted felon join the military?

A More and more people convicted of felonies are turning to military service as a means to a career. Getting a job with a criminal record is tough. Getting a job with a criminal record in a down economy is even tougher. The United States military is finding it tougher to find qualified recruits to fill the country's demands of its foreign policies. Both the Army and Marine Corps have been struggling to increase their numbers as part of a broader effort to meet the combat needs of a military fighting wars in Iraq and Afghanistan. As a result, the number of recruits needing waivers for felony convictions has grown in recent years.

In some cases the military offers waivers to convicted felons making them eligible to serve. In fact the the number of waivers has steadily risen from 2007 to the present.

Typically the crimes that can keep you out of the army are larceny, assault, rape, drug related and murder. There is also consideration for those who have only one conviction and those crimes occurred years ago.

For many felons, this is an opportunity to not only to put their backgrounds behind them find a job, but to learn skills, trades and start careers. The military may hold valuable jobs for felons.

To get more information about waivers for ex-offenders and felons contact your local military recruiter.

JOBS FOR FnELONS - The Illegal Interview Questions
Sample Illegal & Legal Iterview Questions

1. Age
Inappropriate:

How old are you?
What year were you born?
When did you graduate from high school?
Appropriate:
Before hiring, asking if you are over the minimum age for the hours or working conditions.
After hiring, verifying same with a birth certificate or other ID, and asking age on insurance forms.

2.Citizenship
Inappropriate:

Are you a citizen of the US?
Are your parents or spouse citizens of the US?
On what dates did you , your parents or your spouse acquire US Citizenship?
Are you, your parents or your spouse naturalized or native-born US citizens?

Appropriate:

If you are not a US citizen, do you have the legal right to remain permanently in the US?
What is your visa status (if no to the previous question).
Are you able to provide proof of employment eligibility upon hire?

3.Criminal Record
Inappropriate:

Have you ever been arrested?
Have you ever spent a night in jail?

Appropriate:

Have you ever been convicted of a crime?

4.Family
Inappropriate:

Questions concerning spouse, or spouse's employment, salary, arrangements, or dependents.
What kind of child care arrangements have you made?
How will your spouse feel about the amount of time you will be traveling if you get this job?

Appropriate:

Can you work overtime?
Is there any reason you can't start at 7:30am?
Whether an applicant can meet specified work schedules or has activities or commitments that may prevent him or her from meeting attendance requirements.

5.Marital Status
Inappropriate:

Are you married, divorced, separated, engaged, widowed, etc?
Is this your maiden or married name?
What is the name of your relative/spouse/children?
Do you live with your parents?

Appropriate:

After hiring, marital status on tax and insurance forms.

6.Military
Inappropriate:

    What type or condition is your military discharge?
    Can you supply your discharge papers?
 What is your experience in other than US armed forces?

Appropriate:

    Describe the relevant work experience as it relates to this position that you acquired from a US armed forces.

7.National Origin
Inappropriate:

    What is your nationality?
    Where were you born?
    Where are your parents from?
    What's your heritage?
    What is your mother tongue?
    How did you acquire the ability to speak, read or write a foreign language?
    How did you acquire familiarity with a foreign country?
    What language is spoken in your home?
Appropriate:
    Verifying legal U.S. residence or work visa status.
    What languages do you speak, read or write fluently?

8.Parental Status
Inappropriate:

    How many kids do you have?
    Do you plan to have children?
    How old are your children?
    Are you pregnant?
Appropriate:
    After hiring, asking for dependent information on tax and insurance forms.

9.Religion or Creed
Inappropriate:

    What is your religious affiliation?
    Which religious holidays will you be taking off from work?
    Do you attend church regularly?
Appropriate:
    Can you work on Saturdays?

10.Residence
Inappropriate:

    Do you own or rent your home?
    Do you live in town?
    With whom do you live?
Appropriate:

    Inquiries about the address to facilitate contact with the applicant.
    Will you be able to start work at 8:00am

11.Sex
Inappropriate:

    Do you wish to be addressed as Mr., Mrs., Miss, or Ms.?
    What are your plans to have children in the future?
Appropriate:
None

MAJOR COMPANIES THAT HIRE EX-OFFENDERS

AAMCO	COLDWELL BANKER	LA TIMES
ACE HARDWARE	COMPAQ	MACYS
ALAMO RENT A CAR	CONAGRA FOODS	MCDONALDS
ALASKA AIRLINES	DELTA AIRLINES	MOBILE OIL
ALLIED VAN LINES	DELTA FAUCETS	NEW YORK TIMES
AMERICA WEST AIRLINES	DENNYS	NEWSWEEK
AMERICAN AIRLINES	DIAL CORPORATION	NIKE
AMERICAN EXPRESS	DOLE FOODS	PEPSI-CO
AMERICAN GREETINGS	DOLLAR RENT A CAR	PHILLIP MORRIS
APPLE COMPUTER	DOW BRANDS	SARA LEE
AT&T	DUNKIN DONUTS	SHELL OIL
ARCO	DUNLOP TIRES	SHOWTIME NETWORKS
ATLAS VAN LINES	DUPONT CO	SOUTHWEST AIRLINES
AVIS RENT A CAR	DURACELL	SONY
AVON	EDDIE BAUER	SPRINT
BASKIN-ROBBINS	EPSON	TARGET
BEST FOODS	EXXON	TOYS R US
BEST WESTERN	FEDEX	UNITED AIRLINES
BF GOODRICH	FRITO-LAY	VERIZON
BLACK & DECKER	FRUIT OF THE LOOM	WAL-MART
BLUE CROSS BLUE SHIELD	FUJI PHOTO	XEROX
BRIDGESTONE/FIRESTONE	GALOOB TOYS	YAMAHA MOTORS
BRITISH AIRWAYS	GENERAL MILLS	ZENITH ELECTRONICS
BUDGET RENT A CAR	GMAC	
CALKIN KLEIN	GEORGIA-PACIFIC	
CAMPBELL SOUP	HANES HOISERY	
CANON	HILTON	
CARRIER A/C	IBM	
CASIO, INC	K-MART	
COCA-COLA	KRAFT PRODUCTS	

Companies that will hire you on a case by case basis.

1) Wal Mart
2) K Mart
3) Sara Lee
4) McDonalds
5) Best Foods

JOBS for Felons: Companies that Hire Felons - NOT!!!

Alright, for the love of my sanity, please, please, PLEASE stop the madness. Stop sharing these lists that claim these companies hire felons. To the person that is sharing the list, have you verified this information? Have you called everyone on this list and asked what their hiring policy is for convicted felons? If you haven't then you share in the responsibility of spreading false information.

Yes, that is correct. You are spreading something that is not true. Every company has it's own individual policy. Alot of companies do not hire you based on your felony conviction. For those that have been convicted of rape, child molestation, sexual assault, aggravated assault or certain drug crimes, they may never see the likes of being on the payroll of any of these companies. To get their hopes up thinking that they have a chance at employment is just plain wrong.

Crimes of theft, dishonesty and fraud, such as shoplifting, embezzlement, selling or receiving stolen goods and robbery and/or bank robbery have a slim to none chance of working somewhere that takes credit cards or deals with financial information which includes retail. Once again, it is just plain wrong to lump every felon together and give them hope that they can reach out to these companies and have an even playing field. Due diligence will save them time and embarrassment as for many having already been stigmatized as a convicted felon carries much weight.

Help for Ex-offenders and Felons Looking for Jobs

Ex-offenders and Felons can use The Federal Bonding Program to get Jobs

In 1966 the U.S. Department of Labor established The Federal Bonding Program to provide Fidelity Bonds that guarantee honesty for "at-risk", hard-to-place job seekers. The bonds cover the first six months of employment. There is no cost to the job applicant or the employer. In most states the bonds are made available through the state agency responsible for workforce matters.

The Federal Bonding Program is a partnership between the U. S. Department of Labor and Union Insurance Group, an insurance brokerage firm, as agent for Travelers Casualty and Surety Company of America.

Learn all about the program here – www.bonds4jobs.com

So, what can a felon do to gain employment? It's not impossible but it does take time and research. Here is a little something about the law via Buzzle

Employment Laws and Felony Convictions

It is true that some criminal acts authorize the administration to revoke or suspend an individual's right to employment in certain situations, but that doesn't mean you don't get a fair chance to start life afresh merely because of your criminal record. Several states in the US have laws pertaining to employment for felons in place. These laws mainly stress on the fact that an individual cannot be denied employment merely because of prior conviction. Having said that, they do come with some stipulations which may differ from one state to another. These include taking into consideration the severity of the offense, the time elapsed after conviction, etc.

In states like New York, Hawaii, and Minnesota, public employment agencies cannot deny a felon employment unless the crime committed and the job for which he has applied are related directly, or indirectly to each other. Furthermore, if the employer feels that the person is not suitable for the said job because of his conviction, it is mandatory for him to give it in writing. In most of the states, law enforcement agencies, correctional agencies, and jobs that require the person to be in contact with vulnerable population, are kept out of the purview of this law.
Read more at Buzzle: http://www.buzzle.com/articles/companies-that-hire-felons-jobs-that-hire-convicted-felons.html

Sample Resume

Charger Blue

301 Sparkman Drive   256-824-1234
Huntsville, Alabama 35899   chargerblue@uah.edu

EDUCATION

Bachelor of Science in Business Administration   May 2020
University of Alabama in Huntsville   Huntsville, Alabama
Major: Marketing   Minor: Graphic Design   GPA: 3.8/4.0

RELATED COURSEWORK

- Marketing Management – Developed a marketing plan from conception to execution
- Marketing Emerging Technologies – Conducted case studies of how companies effectively develop and market new products

WORK EXPERIENCE

Student Ambassador   May 2011- Present
Office of Admissions- UAHuntsville   Huntsville, Alabama

- Facilitate campus tours for visiting prospective students and families
- Assemble marketing material for campus mailings and events
- Assist with set up of campus preview days
- Enter prospective student data into SCT Banner
- Greet campus visitors and answer general university related questions
- Answer main Admissions telephone and direct calls to the appropriate person
- Assist counselors with various duties relating to recruitment efforts

Cashier   August 2010 - May 2011
Target   Huntsville, Alabama

- Assisted customers at check out
- Counted cash drawer at beginning and end of shift
- Provided and maintained excellent customer service standards set for Target Team Members

TECHNICAL SKILLS

- Microsoft Office
- Adobe Photoshop
- HTML

HONORS AND AFFILATIONS

- Phi Beta Kappa – Honor Society   2010-Present
- Dean's List   2012
- Student Government, Secretary (2012)   2010-2012
- Association of Campus Entertainment, Member   2010-2012

NOTES

NOTES